NATIVE AMERICAN WARS 1622 - 1890

HISTORY FOR KIDS

NATIVE AMERICAN TIMELINES FOR KIDS
6TH GRADE SOCIAL STUDIES

In this book, we're going to talk about the history of the Native American Wars. So, let's get right to it!

When the European settlers first came to America, they encountered natives. The natives had settled in North America thousands of years before and the land was theirs to roam, to hunt, and to call their own. At the beginning, some Native Americans welcomed these new settlers. The new settlers thought they could share their way of life, including their Christian religious beliefs with the Native Americans.

FIRST EUROPEAN SETTLERS

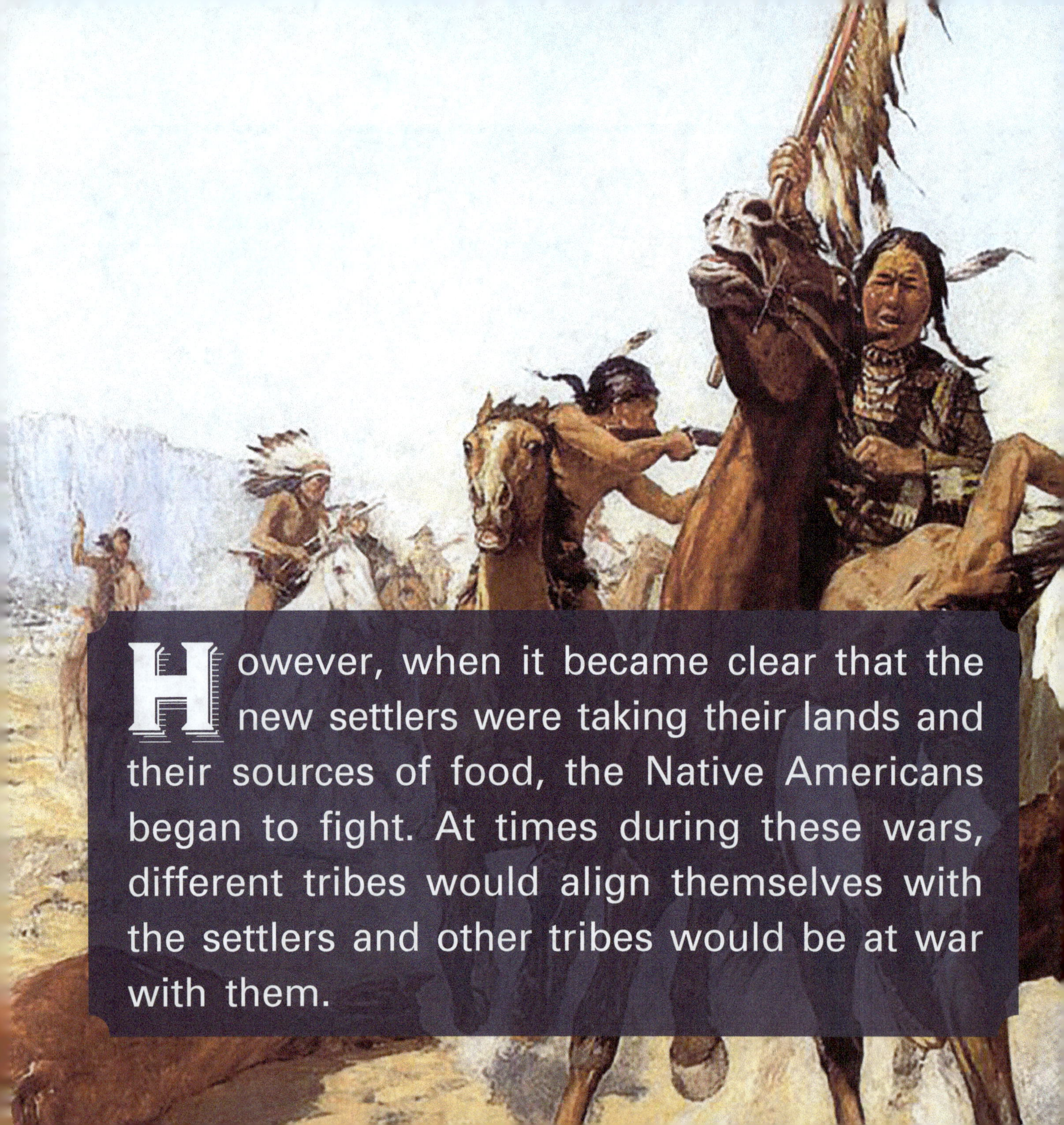

However, when it became clear that the new settlers were taking their lands and their sources of food, the Native Americans began to fight. At times during these wars, different tribes would align themselves with the settlers and other tribes would be at war with them.

here were hundreds of battles between the groups from 1622 to 1890. As the European population spread from east to west, so did the battles between the settlers and the Native Americans. A survey of some of these conflicts follows.

NATIVE AMERICANS MEETING WITH THE SETTLERS

CHIEF POWHATAN AND THE SETTLERS

WARS IN THE 17TH CENTURY

**Powhatan Confederacy
(Virginia, 1622 to 1644)**

The Powhatan Confederacy took place as a series of battles between 1622 and 1644. At the beginning, Chief Powhatan and the 30 Algonquin tribes he commanded were friendly toward the settlers at Jamestown, Virginia.

The Chief showed an interest in the tools the settlers brought with them, but it soon became apparent that both groups would be fighting to stay alive with the available food supply. The chief's daughter, Pocahontas, married a local farmer by the name of John Rolfe and for a while it appeared that tensions had settled down.

POCAHONTAS

However, when Chief Powhatan passed away, the new Chief Opechancanough launched a surprise attack and killed one third of the settlers. Soon thereafter it was all out war. In the year 1632, the tribes were forced to give up a good

portion of the land in the area of Chesapeake Bay. Twelve years later, in the year 1644, over 400 settlers were killed by the Native Americans, but by then, there were enough settlers that the colonies weren't threatened.

Pequot War (Connecticut & Rhode Island, 1637)

There were many tensions between the Native American tribes and the colonists including unethical trading practices by the colonists and the sale of alcohol to the natives. The fact that the livestock from the colonies was destroying the crops grown by the Pequot people was another source of tension.

PEQUOT WAR

In 1636, the Pequot natives killed a dishonest trader by the name of John Oldham. In retaliation, the colonists, along with the Mohegan tribe and the Narragansett tribe, burned a Pequot settlement and killed as many as 700 natives including women and children. Some of the native survivors were sold to slave traders and taken to the island of Bermuda.

King Philip's War (Massachusetts & Rhode Island, 1675 to 1678)

King Philip, who was also known as Chief Metacom, gathered a group of tribes including the Wampanoag and Pocumtuck as well as the Narragansett to fight against the settlers and try to drive them off the lands of New England. It was the last major battle that the Native Americans fought to regain these lands.

KING PHILIP'S WAR

DEATH OF KING PHILIP

Tensions had been sparked by trading partnerships that had collapsed and the fact that settlers were expanding into Native American territories. The bloody battle lasted more than a year until Chief Metacom was captured and killed.

Pueblo Revolt (Arizona & New Mexico, 1680 to 1692)

The Pueblo natives were generally a peaceful people. However, the Spanish had colonized their area and forced them to give up their native religious practices and to convert to Catholicism. A medicine man by the name of Popé led the Pueblo natives along with members of the Apache tribe in an uprising against the Spaniards.

NATIVE AMERICANS BUILDING A SPANISH MISSION

APACHE INDIANS

Over 400 Spaniards were killed and more than 2,000 were driven out by the Native Americans. The natives lived independently for a dozen years before the Spanish came back and re-conquered them.

WARS IN THE 18TH CENTURY

Yamasee War (Southern Region of Carolina, 1715 to 1718)

The Yamasee tribe had been pushed out of their native Florida and Georgia homelands by the Spanish and had moved

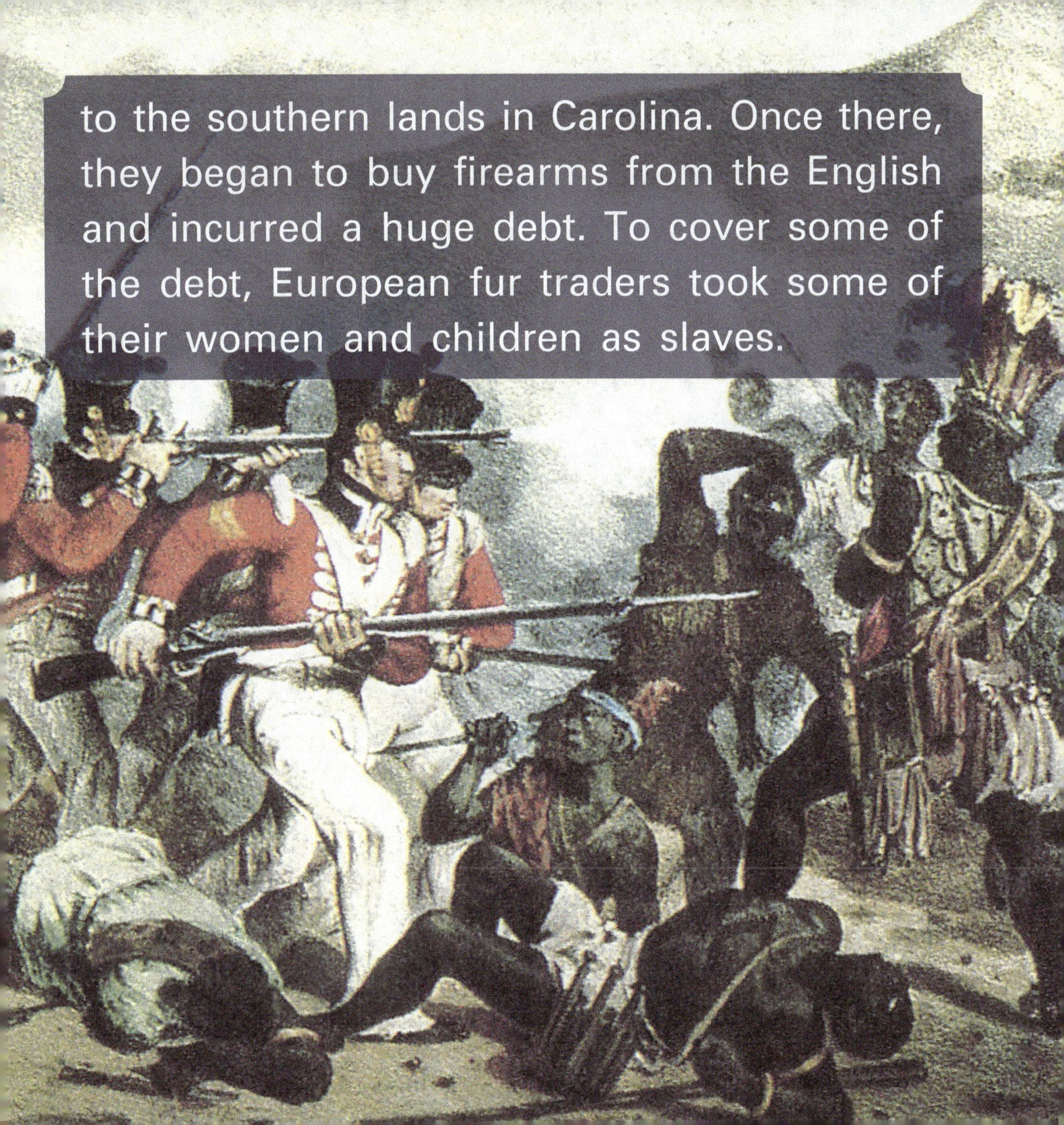
to the southern lands in Carolina. Once there, they began to buy firearms from the English and incurred a huge debt. To cover some of the debt, European fur traders took some of their women and children as slaves.

In 1715, the Yamasee had enough. They formed a federation of natives and attacked. They killed hundreds of settlers, burned homes down, and destroyed the livestock. The Cherokee Native Americans sided with the Carolinians against the Yamasee tribe as did the English settlers in Virginia. If the Carolina settlers hadn't had these reinforcements, their losses would have been even greater. It took almost 10 years for the area to be populated by settlers again.

French and Indian War (Eastern Woodlands in America & Canada, 1754 to 1763)

Despite the name of this war, it was actually French settlers and British settlers who were fighting each other for possession of lands in North America. Both sides had Native American allies. This war was part of the global conflict called the Seven Years War. It was the portion of the conflict that was fought on North American soil.

FRENCH AND INDIAN WAR

The French were aligned with the Algonquin tribes as well as the Shawnee, Ottawa, and others. The British were aligned with the Iroquois tribes as well as the Catawba. The conflict was sparked when the French built a fort on the Ohio River. After nine years of fighting, Britain won the war and France had to relinquish its territories in that region. Britain now owned the land to the east of the Mississippi and Spain owned the land to the west.

Pontiac's Conspiracy
(Ohio River Valley, 1763)

For the most part, the Native Americans had had a good relationship with the French. The French were generally fair traders and had been able to live in peace with the Native Americans. The natives had been able to keep their lands when the French were in charge. However, now that the British had won the French and Indian War, they began to expand into the native lands.

VISIT OF CHIEF PONTIAC TO THE FRENCH

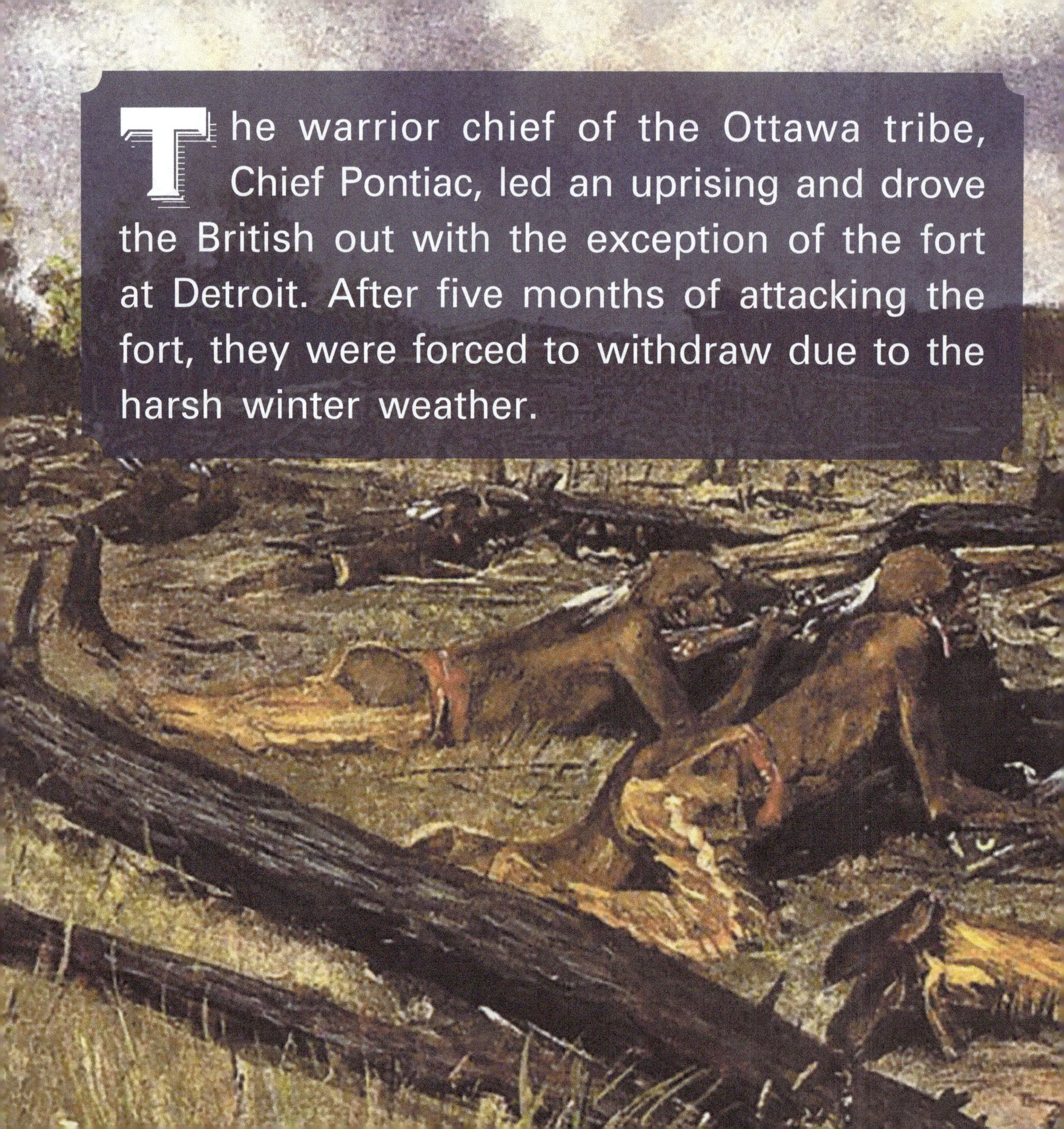
The warrior chief of the Ottawa tribe, Chief Pontiac, led an uprising and drove the British out with the exception of the fort at Detroit. After five months of attacking the fort, they were forced to withdraw due to the harsh winter weather.

SIEGE OF FORT DETROIT

Lord Dunmore's War
(Southern Ohio River Valley, 1774)

After the negotiations of the French and Indian War, the British had stated that no more settlers would move into areas that were west of the Appalachian Mountain range. However, the settlers from Virginia and other areas ignored this agreement and kept moving into Native American territories. This led to war. Lord Dunmore, the governor of the Virginia colony dispatched 3,000 soldiers and was victorious against over 1,000 natives of the Mingo and Shawnee tribes.

LORD DUNMORE

TECUMSEH

WARS IN THE 19TH CENTURY

Battle of Tippecanoe (Indiana, 1811)

Two Shawnee leaders, Tecumseh and his brother Tenskwatawa, also known as the Prophet, wanted to drive the white settlers out of the Indiana territory. They believed that the "Master of Life" would aid them in their desire to defeat the settlers if they gave up all of the customs that the white men had brought with them including weapons and tools.

Many natives followed the Prophet's beliefs. They thought that bullets from the guns of the white man wouldn't hurt them if they followed what the Master of Life had revealed to the Prophet. William Henry Harrison, who would later be President of the United States, led an army to the Native American village located at what is the city of West Lafayette in Indiana today.

WILLIAM HENRY HARRISON

BATTLE OF TIPPECANOE

The Prophet and his men attacked, but were defeated by Harrison's troops. There were heavy losses on both sides. Harrison and his men burned the village to the ground and the natives turned away from the Prophet after this defeat. This battle was later named the Battle of Tippecanoe.

First, Second, and Third Seminole Wars (Florida)

These three conflicts were fought between the army of the United States and the Seminole Native Americans who lived in Florida. These three wars were the most expensive, both in terms of money spent and human lives lost, of all the Native American wars. They also lasted the longest.

ATTACK OF THE SEMINOLES ON THE BLOCK HOUSE

SEMINOLE WAR IN EVERGLADES

he first was from 1816 to 1819, the second was from 1835 to 1842, and the third was from 1855 to 1858. The Seminoles were pushed back into the southern Everglades swamps of Florida, where some natives still live.

Battle of the Little Bighorn (Montana, 1876)

When gold was discovered in the Black Hills, white prospectors began to move into the area and the Sioux Native Americans began to attack them. In this famous battle, also called "Custer's Last Stand" famous Civil War hero George A. Custer decided to attack Sioux Native Americans who were gathered at the Little Bighorn River in Montana. He underestimated the number of Native Americans there and he and his 250 men were killed.

BATTLE OF THE LITTLE BIGHORN

GHOST DANCE

The Wounded Knee Massacre
(South Dakota, 1890)

By 1890, the Native Americans had lost their way of life against the expansion of the white man. Many of them began a new form of religion called the "Ghost Dance." They believed that if they participated in these ritualistic dances with their accompanying songs that their way of life could be revived. The United States military saw this as a precursor to war.

They arrested the famous chief, Sitting Bull. A fight occurred and Sitting Bull was killed. A group of Sioux Native Americans led by Chief Big Foot camped at the reservation at Pine Ridge. The United States cavalry arrived and when the natives began to dance a tense situation occurred and it led to gunfire. At the end of the battle, over 150 Native Americans had been killed including women and children.

SITTING BULL

SUMMARY

When the European settlers first arrived in North America, they thought the Native Americans could share their resources and be converted to Christianity. However, it soon became apparent that the Europeans planned to expand throughout North America. This expansion would threaten the lands, culture, and food sources of the Native Americans. To complicate the situation, many Native American tribes were enemies so they sometimes sided with the settlers to help eliminate their enemies.

Now that you've read about the history of the Native American Wars you may want to read about the mystery behind one of the first colonies in America in the Baby Professor book, The Mystery of the Lost Colony of Roanoke - History 5th Grade | Children's History Books.

NATIVE AMERICANS OF THE COLUMBIA PLATEAU

Visit

BABY PROFESSOR
EDUCATION KIDS

www.BabyProfessorBooks.com

to download Free Baby Professor eBooks
and view our catalog of new and exciting
Children's Books